# Free Verse Editions

Edited by Jon Thompson

# DISMANTLING THE ANGEL

WINNER OF THE NEW MEASURE POETRY PRIZE

## Eric Pankey

Parlor Press
Anderson, South Carolina
www.parlorpress.com

Parlor Press LLC, Anderson, South Carolina, 29621

Printed in the United States of America
S A N: 2 5 4 - 8 8 7 9


Library of Congress Cataloging-in-Publication Data

Pankey, Eric, 1959-
  [Poems. Selections]
  Dismantling the Angel / Eric Pankey.
       pages cm
  "Winner of the New Measure Poetry Prize."
  ISBN 978-1-60235-487-6 (pbk. : acid-free paper) -- ISBN 978-
1-60235-488-3 (adobe ebook) -- ISBN 978-1-60235-489-0 (ibook)
-- ISBN 978-1-60235-490-6 (epub) -- ISBN 978-1-60235-491-3
(kindle)
  I. Title.
  PS3566.A575A6 2014
  811'.54--dc23
                                        2013042186


Cover design by David Blakesley.
Cover art: "February 09, 2012," by Paolo Ventura. Used by
  permission of the artist.



Printed on acid-free paper.

Parlor Press, LLC is an independent publisher of scholarly and
trade titles in print and multimedia formats. This book is available
in paperback and ebook formats from Parlor Press on the World
Wide Web at http://www.parlorpress.com or through online and
brick-and-mortar bookstores. For submission information or to
find out about Parlor Press publications, write to Parlor Press,
3015 Brackenberry Drive, Anderson, South Carolina, 29621, or
email editor@parlorpress.com.

# Contents

*Perhaps an angel looks like everything*
*We have forgotten, I mean forgotten*
*Things that don't seem familiar when*
*We meet them again, lost beyond telling,*
*Which were ours once.*

—John Ashbery

# DISMANTLING THE ANGEL

# Dismantling the Angel

Put each feather, quill point down, in its own Mason jar, sprinkle in paper ash and table salt, and place each jar in a root cellar, refrigerator, or cooler. As one does in an autopsy, make a *Y* incision from the back of the ears, meeting at the sternum, and then down the chest. There should be no bleeding. Fold back the flesh, which by now will feel like vellum. Remove the heart and liver. You will find no bones and no other organs. You will find the heart where you expect to find it, packed in straw, canvas fibers, millet, and crushed cowry shells. The heart, as dull and heavy as slag, can be used to hold a door open. The liver—green, made of malachite smelted in a coal-fired kiln—can be ground to sand, or dissolved in salt water and distilled, making a whiskey to warm the winter. The appendages—the arms, the legs, and the wing-hinges—are useless and should be stacked with the cordwood. They burn easily but add no heat to the fire, no brilliance to the flame. The little drops remaining on the cutting table look like dried blood but are in fact gall-stained paraffin. Scraped up, melted and recast, they make lousy candles. They are best used as a sealing wax or as a suitable lubricant for pipefittings. If you have not done so, put each feather, quill point down, in its own Mason jar, sprinkle in paper ash and table salt, and place each jar in a root cellar, refrigerator, or cooler. This is important, thus I repeat myself. Left overnight at room temperature, each feather can regenerate an entire angel, all the feathers a holy host.

I.

# The Kingdom of Smoke

A man has two sons. The younger, having asked for and been refused his inheritance, leaves, saying, "If I were to speak one more word, if I were to complete one more sentence, I could not avoid the predicate's tragic turn."

Angered, the elder son yells at his brother in farewell, "A crow flies as the crow flies. You are brother now to crows. The crow's curse is its caw, the sweep of its coal-black wing."

What is a father to do? Wear his shame like a splint and a sling? The two halves of his land are divided and held together by a thicket's bent vertebrae.

He drops a match into the thorn-tangle and soon his is a kingdom of smoke. Looking back, the younger son sees the blaze but continues away: a long stretch of road behind him, a longer stretch ahead— wind-worn, sleet-skulked, perhaps impassable.

I admit I was not privy to the garbled argument between the elder son and the father, silhouetted by flames, but I witnessed the dumb show and shadow-play skirmish of their gestures.

Flushed and scattered by fire, crows above the twin fields resolved as an as-of-yet indiscernible genus of randomness.

# The Talismanic Shirt

The cotton of the shirt—tight-knit, impenetrable by sunlight, yet somehow airy—did not reveal the thousand and one scriptures inked in minute, almost illegible handwriting on the shirt's inside: down the sleeves, across the back and on either side of the mother of pearl buttons from collar to tails. Radiant, the shirt shone as if its own source of light. To *see* the shirt was to be in its presence, to be illuminated by it. Whether the universe opened or closed did not matter. *White*, if *white* exists at all, could not be exemplified better than by the shirt. If one opened the illustrated dictionary to *white*, there would be the shirt in miniature. If one opened the illustrated dictionary to *shirt*, there would be the shirt glowing, glaring, flaring, shining, glistering in miniature. I have worn the shirt. Perhaps to say *I have worn the shirt* is too common a way to express it. It was not as if I pulled a black turtleneck over my head and watched the play of static, not as if I had put one arm and then another into a blazer as the tailor brushed something off my shoulder to say, *there, that's just right*. In the shirt, I was neither subject nor object. The shirt on me was the subject and the object. Do not mistake the shirt for some childhood dream of an invisibility cloak. Riddles, enigmas, conundrums and tables open before the shirt, open easily like the paper of a garlic clove beneath the blade. Far from invisible, I stood out in a crowd. Normally polite children pointed. Men and women shielded their eyes as if I were naked, as if I stood there naked and then had become even more naked. The teenagers on the corner couldn't be bothered, which is to say they took note but would not let on to one another. No one envies the wearer of the shirt. The shirt is there: clean, pressed, and ready to wear. I gave it up once, which is to say: it is there: clean, pressed, and ready to wear. At night in the closet on a common wire hanger, the shirt vibrates like a struck lightning rod. I listen to its low hum. I listen to the swarm of scripture inside the shirt calm as if the late dark were a drowse of smoke.

# Fire and Wind

Even Jesus was a trickster. He did not appear as he was, but he appeared so that he could be seen. Hard not to admire the scrutiny it takes to adhere to a body—blunt, burdened, breakable—when unconsuming fire and wind (which feeds such a flame and draws it up into a pillar) are one's habit. To the lame, he hobbled on a crutch. To the poor, he was the poorest man. Scholars argued with him over the law. No one knew he spoke in riddles. On the day of the harvest, the weeds, plainly visible, were gathered and burned. To the sower, he was a gardener. For the carpenter, he held the plumb bob. With the arsonist, he set a blaze.

# Autobiography of Fire

The fire retains only its shape, its shifting, ambiguous, wind-shredded shape.

A bevy of flames. Sparks splayed beneath a sledgehammer. Bonfires at midsummer. Pentecostal tongues. Banked embers. *Meteors fright the fixed stars of heaven.* The charred body of Osiris as spent fuel. Signal fire built from a shipwreck. A thumb-struck match flaring. A fire kindled with Cain's offering.

Prior to words: the inarticulateness of fire, a long mumbled sentence through the hardwood forest, down the mountain, to the seaside dunes, where it shushed its way through the sparse grasses.

][brimstone and *fire* from the LORD out of heaven][he took the *fire* in his hand, and a knife][Behold the *fire* and the wood: but where is the lamb for a burnt offering][in a flame of *fire* out of the midst of a bush][the bush burned with *fire*, and the bush was not consumed] [the *fire* ran along upon the ground][and *fire* mingled with the hail, very grievous][with *fire*, and unleavened bread; and with bitter herbs][

Having consumed the Library at Alexandria, the flames remained tongue-tied, mute.

Fire like poppies in the wheat. Poppies like fire in the wheat.

][his eyes were as a flame of *fire*][ like unto a flame of *fire*][ gold tried in the *fire*, that thou mayest be rich][ seven lamps of *fire*][ And the angel took the censer, and filled it with *fire* of the altar][ and *fire* mingled with blood][ a great mountain burning with *fire*]  [having breastplates of *fire*, and of jacinth, and brimstone][ by the *fire*, and by the smoke, and by the brimstone, which issued out of their mouths][

The fire retains only its shape, its shifting, ambiguous, wind-shredded shape.

# Parable of the Empty Jar

A certain woman carried a jar full of milled grain. While she was walking on the road, still some distance from home, one of the handles of the jar broke and the grain emptied out behind her on the road. When she reached her house, she set the jar down and found it empty. As she set out again to fill the jar, she noticed a flock of birds lined all along the road feeding. From her house to the mill where she had purchased the grain, one bird after another took flight before her footsteps. "I've never seen birds feed with such a hunger," she said to the miller as he refilled her jar and took her coins. "A cold winter must be coming," he said, "As cold as hell." "I thought hell was a fiery pit," she said. "It is," he replied, "but we feel it as ice to our marrow. Imagine how it would be for a bird which is hollow-boned." As she walked home, the grain spilled and one bird after another landed behind her to feed. When she reached her house, she set the jar down and found it empty. There was no wood in the stove, no oil in the lamp. The cupboards held only dust. "A cold winter, indeed," she said as she started down the road to the mill, this time wrapped in a shawl, and the flock twisted up before her like a pillar of smoke.

# The Expulsion

We found the snakeskin snagged among thorns in the cutback thicket. Wind off the water filled it and it roused. The serpent's slough did not call forth slither or sibilance, did not embody headlong knowledge of falter and fracture. We remembered then the season of the blackberry—all thorn and seed and a little flesh—remembered the overripe pear's cloy collapsed in its sugar's murk. Autumn, deep in its own wax, guttered and waned. We backtracked through a labyrinth of stories, through laughter that laughter kindled, but found no lucid wound. Nonetheless, we sutured one day coarsely to the next. The hours, stored and storied in taxonomies, could not hold, in the end, what they displaced: the scrape and scuff of gravel beneath our feet, the roadside oats rust-blighted, the *to-be-named* there at a remove, already hearsay, already secondhand. The constellations above— mediated by categories, by principles of collation—were mute, not mutable, and the past—carbon and silica wind partakes of and in—scattered.

# The House of Lazarus

In Caravaggio's "The Raising of Lazarus," Lazarus appears to fall: body taut with rigor at a forty-five degree angle to the stone floor, caught in the arms of a bystander, who wonder-struck, looks away from Jesus and into the victim's face, as do Lazarus's sisters who set the story in motion out of grief, with the best of intentions, as if this dead man alive still could be their brother and not a stranger shadowed by tomb-stench and bad luck, a stranger they must feed and dress. And who never sleeps. They hear him at night pouring out the jar of lentils, one by one dropping each in the jar, counting out loud, pouring them out again, counting again, the number different each time although nothing's changed at all, except the hour which gets late until it's early, when everyone else in the house gives in, gives up on sleep.

# Essay on the Entry into Jerusalem

*Here*—the terminus from which he begins. The road, tilted like a tipped-up tile, points to those in trees pulling down branches. Wind rucks and buckles the cloak-covered path. Soon enough the day will be a ruin. Soon the crisp half-light of dusk will give way to the salt-light of stars, a gibbous moon. Although foretold, the future is the past: a leaden, inert matter-of-factness. His retinue approaches like a storm. Lightning blinds us for now. His afterimage is that of a ghost.

# A Study for a Figure at the Base of the Crucifixion

It is hard to recall what she did not know before she knelt here: the brayed past smudged from too much handling.

Crows, like ghosts flocked in a field of asphodels, gather.

They startle up in the air, drop like a length of chain.

She hears their cold caws as lamentation, as laughter.

Who can speak about tomorrow, forsaken before it arrives?

Was there once a room ablaze in sunlight, dust motes flashing around him as exhausted he collapsed beside her?

The constellations turn, distorted by dark matter, shimmer and roil like a catch as a net is hauled in.

## Essay on Mannerism

Not a cave's absolute dark, but more like char, ash-scrim, the chirr
and clicks of starlings, dusk-tinged, a crag of coal, this black we call
*black* as if a word might be offered as proxy: black like the petrified
heart of a lamb, like the posture of grief the figure embodies in Rosso
Fiorentino's 1521 "Deposition"—hunched, hunkered, harrowed—
with his (her?) back to the cross.

# Essay on the Supper at Emmaus

Once recognized, he disappears, not into the *was* or *will be,* but into the *unalways*: the nothing, the plump emptiness of zero.

You say his name, but the word will not adhere.

# Ordinary Time: Watching Starlings

Balanced on an axis of symmetry, the flock unfurls. The flock—an endless anagram, a quiver and black-flash reflected on a flooded grave's flat surface—recongregates. The flock—singular, plural—postpones, for now, the moment and its duration (the way ordinary time withholds miracle and crisis, withholds the clarity that is the aftermath of catharsis). The flock breaks, musters, banks, collapses like a torn sail. Then, with the rush of a millrace, the flock lifts into a wind-cricked and leafless tree, idles like a noisy engine into evening.

# Short Sentence

The soul enters the flesh and, in the crossing, is fed and threshed as a
flame is fed and threshed by wind; the soul inhabits its unruly body,
abides the abject, bides the time of its short sentence, for now, for the
promise of a bodiless ever after.

# The Daughters of Lot

*after Carlo Carra*

We are lost: the destination, it seems, has been misplaced.

Trails switchback up the foothills, snarl at the summit.

We speak as one voice from a mutual vantage point.

We speak with two voices, back to back: echoes wrought by distance, by time.

In the well, we find only depth, only hours muddled by wine.

How many tons of tailings for the thin bronze of our bangles?

How many times can our four hands exchange the frayed string of a cat's cradle?

The city, ravaged by flame, heals over with nettles and bindweed.

As flood water channels into fields, a burnt trunk exudes perfumed resin.

After much racket, the crows leave, appeased, or so it seems, but by what?

# Tableau from the Last Days

Oxcarts haul the plague-stricken to the outskirts. What light remains is pitted against the murk, coruscates on sores and suppurations. In a city of funerals, church bells clang, erase the hours. Clouds writhe like a brazen serpent. Oxen kick up dust. Each pile of dirt fits the dug hole beside it. The not-yet-sick stand in line to be measured for caskets, although lumber is in short supply and the carpenter's son is stacked there on the cart. If the driver falls ill, the ox, it seems, knows the way.

# Tomb Furnishings

Ark of river stone.

Ashen residue of straw.

Attic dust, cellar damp.

Calabash adorned with cowries.

A conundrum, a compendium.

Corrosives that free an image.

Dried seed-heads, boluses, antlers among the tangled roots.

Dusk pinned down on a stony draw.

Folio volumes of maps and anagoges.

Gaps in the narrative where coincidence enters.

The half of speech that is the listener's.

Joists, beams, floorboards.

Loams and siennas.

The lure of light.

Models of earthly and heavenly palaces.

The moment's spur.

Nest the wind picks apart.

A pause, a rest.

Sound of waters coming together.

Stupa of rain.

Sufficient repetition to suggest endlessness.

Thrown voices, thrown shadows.

Tool-marks on the overgrown knots, char on the cross grain.

Tress of hair.

Vectors and quadrants.

Verdict written in sand.

II.

# Essay on a Lemon

Like a lens, the lemon clarifies by way of distortion. Like a mirror, the lemon implies an unseen onlooker. The lemon, transformed by one's attention to it, is a spark pent up in a barn, is tenuous auroral light, is long shadows on a glacier. The lemon waits to be recognized like the inscrutable event of a miracle. The lemon is like a nail before the hammer's invention. One experiences the mystical as the phenomenal. Note how easily, with the vessel of the body broken, one ascends. The lemon is an anagram, a quicksilver sliver of memory, countless sparrows alighting on a swimming stag's rack. Like Man Ray's "Indestructible Object," the lemon had to be remade. To make one is really quite easy: *Cut out the eye from a photograph of one who has been loved but is seen no more. Attach the eye to the pendulum of a metronome and regulate the weight to suit the tempo desired. Keep going to the limit of endurance. With a hammer well aimed, try to destroy the whole at a single blow.*

## Lunar Calendar

The moon is a midwife who delivers a bundle of salt.

The moon sheds a spring-fed light, white as the limestone in Galena, Illinois.

The moon is a knuckle gashed to the bone.

The moon rescinds its blessing, rests its forehead on a crosier of walrus ivory.

The moon is magnetite, a precipitate of iron and oxygen.

The moon is a June bug larva.

The moon snags the train of its wedding dress in the blackberry brambles.

The moon is the pale-bellied mole: lame, hobbled, all maw.

The moon inhales the sluggish cloy of opium, exhales gypsum dust.

The moon is a geode, a glacial erratic, a sinkhole.

The moon is a window opaque with reflection.

The moon, fluent in every tongue, remains mum.

# Epic Fragment

To make distance legible, a single taper in a candelabrum [
[                                                                                      ]
                                        ] A blur and bundle of shadows
the mirror snares and hoards [                                                         ]
[                                                                                      ]
[        ]The wrecked table, scraps cast aside, strewn[                                ]
The bow drawn taut. The last arrow, unreleased[                                        ]
[                                                                                      ]
[                       ] Penelope's suitors dead [                                    ]
[                                                                                      ]
[                                        ]The milk of figs on his lips[                ]

## Nineteen Essays

Birds fall like stars fell illuminating Lucifer's tumble. Birds fall out of trees and speak in a wild plumage of voices.

: :

The stained and slackened wallpaper is torn, mottled, and defaced. The abandoned house is now an abode of spirits and rain.

: :

One must verify, in a dream, useless, dissonant data by means of a slide-rule and puddled moonlight in mussel shells.

: :

On the stones of the plague market, one leaves coins in limewater and finds on the rocks the next day cheese, cider, and coarse flour.

: :

A fat, pink, beribboned pig circumambulates to enclose a profane space, to usher in an age of banality.

: :

By the time you count from one to ten, this trickle—a creek—will have carved out the thousand strata of a ravine.

: :

In an anatomical study of the swooning Virgin, Mary is held hostage by the dead weight of the pressing moment.

: :

My wife wants to pre-decease me. She's picked a replacement wife perfect for me. The catch? The new wife's husband has got to go.

: :

This accretion you call the *self*—errors, fuck-ups, some good luck—reminds you you have learned to say nothing at last concisely.

: :

Translucent. Barely there. The risen Christ casts no shadow. What drama but violence? What violence but wilderness?

: :

Over the years we have surveyed each other's body in touch as we fell into dream, the blurred borders of self crossed over.

: :

In a purification ritual, twin winged-deities sprinkle pollen upon the Tree of Life, then open the gate.

: :

The uncarved pumpkin is numinous at dusk, an accident of light and disruptions of light—keen, enkindled, all aglow.

: :

Vulcan works the hammer and anvil, Zephyrus the bellow: all dark matter possesses the stark gravity of lost time.

: :

Pregnant with annunciation, the angel cannot enter. The senseless sublime is deciphered only by the senses.

: :

Each thought in my head is like smoke in a bell jar: arabesques, curlicues, blown rings that shed their substance, collapse as fine ash.

: :

What is the name of the reckless game by which the world is built and destroyed, restored and toppled, harrowed, sown, and harvested?

: :

The observations, recorded with scrupulous precision, conclude the blood is a pigment of lead and buckthorn berries.

: :

River stones, scars of erosion marks: we feel light and open our eyes to light—stolen fire—which is the beginning of form.

# The Equilibrium of a Swan's Feather

Alive, no doubt, with the low voltage that runs through a dowsing rod, the swan relinquishes its *swan-ness*. The swan vanishes. Or, at least, on the continuum of visible light, the *what-was* pulses ultraviolet. One might, in response, write an equation regarding the pull of parallel distances, of one disembodied notion upon another. One word salvaged from the obsolete, maybe two, might be all that is needed, (if *need* can be used here to mean *desire*) to offset the swan-reflection where the swan is no more.

# Film Still

*after Douglas Gordon*

As if on the surface of the moon, cold in light and shadow, time itself is outmoded—all glints, struck flints, mica flares—like TV static, the fluorescent hum of the exit booth in long term parking, or at the turnpike's end, and if the future seems permeated with foreboding, imagine the landscape unfurling behind, a blurry rear-projection, without soundtrack, without the windshield wipers' tick, or the on-again, off-again rain, imagine the driver's eye as dark water down a drain and the past seems a momentary misdeed, a modicum, a mote washed away by a tear.

# Variations on a Theme

The picture Norman Bates moves aside to access a peephole in order to peer into Marion's room and watch her undress, before he enters that room later, dressed as his mother, to stab the naked Marion to death in her shower, is a cheaply framed, dusty print of "Susanna and the Elders," a popular subject for painters—a nude woman looked upon without her knowing, except in that version of the story she is saved in the end from the death a gaze initiated.

: :

He was doing his dishes. Seven o'clock on a winter evening. He looked out his apartment's kitchen window, a little fogged from the hot water, and across the alley he saw through her uncurtained window his neighbor step out of her bathroom into her bedroom, naked, a towel turbaned on her head, another towel in hand. He watched her through the frame of the window beyond which she never moved as she dried and dressed, as if his looking held her in view. From that night on seven o'clock was the time to do the dishes.

: :

He tries to be in bed first, so he can watch his wife undress, apply her lotions, let down her hair, move back and forth across the room as she attends her nighttime tasks. That is why he keeps his glasses on: to see, to watch. And to not seem to be watching. To be allowed a stolen glance. After thirty years, the erotic still walks that tightrope between the *allowed* and the *stolen*. What, he wonders guiltily, does he mean by *allowed*, by *stolen*.

: :

Jimmy Stewart, a photographer, has a broken leg and passes his time in a wheelchair at his window with a telephoto lens observing the lives of his neighbors. His girlfriend and housekeeper at first do not approve. When one looks, one will almost always see something one had better not have seen. And once seen, how then to *unsee* it? How not to multiply it in memory, to fret over it, to imagine perhaps that you saw even more than you remembered? Given that we remember so little, isn't it amazing how just a glimpse can set a story in motion? When, later, Raymond Burr breaks into Stewart's apartment to kill him, it is only by setting off flash bubs, thus blinding Burr, that Stewart manages, crippled as he is, to survive.

# The Inner Workings

That which startles, bores us as well, announces likeness and difference, pinpoints the *now* while the mind meanders, and even then the illegible, perhaps even the unspeakable, unblurs like heat into a mirage.

Francis Bacon once said, "I want to bring about the sensation of the thing without the boredom of its conveyance."

In an eighteenth-century etching, a figure stands naked by a tree. His face conveys nothing of pain. The flayed flesh is pinned back to reveal the gut-work, the heart, the rungs of ribs. Arms held wide for an unencumbered view.

# Two Children Threatened by a Nightingale

*after Max Ernst*

Attentive as one is to a whisper, the children wade through standing water, uncertain of its depth or source. They find and salvage a sunbleached, rain-wet train schedule. For their short lives the depot has been boarded shut. He has a flair for death and can fashion a noose from corn silk. She keeps an archive of diaries. She is the movie extra a camera seeks out, lingers on. He reads the subtitles aloud before the characters speak. She imagines sleep to be a furnished room. He imagines sleet on the rolled hay, the must of empty stables, the tin-edge of blood on the tongue. By schema and classifications, they are a sister and a brother. Waylaid between this puddle and the next, she creates a theory of the spectral. He fingers through a cache of candies. He is plump and ready for the oven. She could not even flavor a stockpot. She is the overlooked subject. She deciphers a language of mishearings. They cling to the hitherto unknown. When they dissect the bird they find nothing of the song.

# A Man on Whom the Sun Goes Down

*After your labors, will you return?*

No. My luck is so thin it leaves a paper-cut.

*Can you not see the glory that is yours for the asking?*

No. Reflection is a trap, a snare, a view a surface affords. Consider what the swallows score on the air. Nothing. Not even a trace.

*Did you come empty-handed?*

No. I brought my own indigenous loneliness. I brought my fate entangled in the remote, ancient light of stars. I brought oracle bones that when tossed read again and again "bull in a quagmire."

*Will you not toss the oracle bones again?*

No.

*Look. Is that your ship that founders at the horizon?*

No. That is just the sun going down.

# The Worst Fears of the Emperor

The temple offerings untouched even by the flies. Rumors of plague. The face of the soothsayer, as white as a wound unbandaged, when they drag her drowned and bloated from the canal. The bit taut in the mouth of a horse fallen in battle. A time of siege. The dog as it snaps its jaw in a dream. Not the cease-fire, not the retreat, not the body count, but the conditions of the treaty, the redrawn map without rivers, vineyards, or summer palace. The debauchery of the clergy in their fidelity to God. The frozen inkwell that delays a decree. Venereal disease and its cure: mercury vapors, the lance, and the cautery. The slain courier who carried the names of the conspirators. The aftermath of clemency. The unknown assailant. A fire in the granary. A fire in the stables. Saturn eclipsed. The viceroy secretly tutoring the bastard son to forge a signature, to conceal a pistol, to parry and thrust. The owl at daybreak. The owl at noon.

# Underworld Variations

The lovers make a monster of themselves—

Mutable, serpentine, torturous, flexed—

Neither one thing nor another, nor two—

Intertwined, attenuated, disheveled—

A wreath of wings, a hawk harried by crows—

    : :

Not lovers, but a rape, a woman ripped—

Swept in a god's arms up, wronged and away—

Trampled hyacinths, poppies, and meadowsweets—

Plum blossoms ghosted, ghosted in snow—

The moment dilates; the moment contracts—

    : :

On a papyrus fragment, a list of the gifts he gave as bribes—

An incised ivory wand, a twin gazelle diadem, terebinth resin—

A throne of sweet cedar shade, an empty leather quiver—

For a groom's gift she gave him the one thing she carried from above—

A needle that once sewed a shroud—

: :

More a root cellar than a palace, the space is cramped—

Bride and groom, grub and clay, they lie together till spring—

He holds her as a grave holds a body, not coldly—

But without passion, matter-of-fact-ly, one might say—

Time passes so slowly here the flames are carved marble—

# Owl

Owl (oul) n. [ME owle<OE ule] 1. Rain on a scythe. 2. A hem of water around one's waist. 3. Autumn marked by an *x* where *x* can equal the renunciation of memory or that which is impervious to interpretation. 4. A seed placed on the tongue of the deceased. 5. Sparks splayed beneath a sledge. <Through the blacksmith shop the *owl* flew.> 6. The way the divine penetrates the material. 7. The experience of loss although nothing is missing; mute stupor; black bile. 8. A discarded yet imperishable garment snagged on a branch. <Look, there is an *owl* in the sycamore.>

# After Li Ho

It is not long before pleasure bores, before you look up and see the river's water shivered by wind.

As always, the uncanny returns us to the moment, which is to say, to the ordinary, the contradictions and anomalies.

Paths zigzag up a cliffside, where the rope of a waterfall hangs.

The moon's jade crumbles beneath its own weight.

I come from the Midwest by which I mean *the sky weighing down on all sides*, storms latent in the convergence of air masses, tornado weather: a sickle whetted in a shed full of hornets.

Like you, I've looked for answers in fox tracks.

Once leaving the movies, I looked up and saw a homeless man dressed in an old suit I'd given to the Salvation Army, and was surprised to note how good the outfit looked on such a lean figure.

I should loose some weight, I thought, and worried I had been hasty giving the suit away.

# How to Make Love to Someone
# You Do Not Love

Say your lover's name over and over again as if an incantation. Say
the name until it loses all meaning, until all you hear are plosives,
liquids, and aspirations. Keep in mind that lovemaking like a poem is
an ephemeral exploration. If you find yourself tempted by affection,
think: O, the tedious repetitions of the avant-garde! O, the endless
integers for which the variable $n$ is a stand-in! Recall, if you must, the
root meaning of *autopsy*: *aut-* (self) + *opsis* (to see)—that is, to see the
self, to decipher the self, to render the self. See your lover as you see
yourself: fuel for the fire, a mere spark in a conflagration. A kiss will
betray your insincerity, so kiss at your own risk. If you find yourself
distracted think: O, quiet of ruins! O, cool of the evening! O, the
twin gazelles of her breasts!

# Ox

The onion grass and the sweet grass are chewed the same—again, efficiently. And it is that care—the sure thoroughness, the calm depending as much on the beast's weight as it does on will, the slow circuit its blood takes—that we admire. The ox does not care for the twenty words we've saved for it. It does not care that steadiness is its burden. In its dull language, the ox says little. If it chose to mock us it would do so with such a subtlety that we'd miss it as we raised a whip or pitched moldy hay from the sharpened tines of a fork. *Here,* we'd say. *Here. This is for you alone. Here.*

# III.

# The Inheritance

A pack of cigarettes—its foil square torn open—and a pistol—a German Luger—in the top drawer amid handkerchiefs, knee socks, and underwear. In the bathroom, a ring of rust bled from beneath the shaving cream can. A lip of oily dust sealed the wall-slot for used razor blades. The gold cuff link in the ashtray did not match the one fallen behind the nightstand. Each of the shirts in the closet had buttoned sleeves. A pressed corsage, its pink leached out, left a stain, a pale watermark, on the Bible's crinkled pages. Still stuck in the rose's green taped stem: a pin. Marked on the back of a photo in pencil: *Kyoto, Japan: 1947*. The soldier, my father, younger than I am now, squints back against the flash.

# Relics and Kindling

*I can't understand you when you mumble*, my father would say, and look, I've spent my entire life mumbling.

The random details equal the whole of our attention to them: our delight in connections, our tedium at the impasse; our delight at the impasse, our tedium in the connections.

High in the maple amid the keys and the wind, I'd sway as the branch tipped, tossed, shivered and swooned, and if not for my grip, the gray bark against my cheek, the tether of gravity and my own fear of heights, I swear I flew: above the housetops and the field, above the gully flooded with runoff, the spiral of swifts (for years I thought they were bats) lifting from the incinerator's brick chimney, above the powder blue water tower, a tear-mark of rust beneath each rivet, above the grain elevators of North Kansas City and the wide Missouri, above barges and high tension wires, above bluff and scree, and flying—my body not my own: not a changeling's body, not a projection against a screen, not a fall from which I would wake with a thud on box-springs—the shuddered fabric of my windbreaker caught a gust like a sail as I stepped out onto air and for a moment dropped like the swifts as they bob and swoop down and downward, only to shoot up and out of sight.

Awake, I would listen for the inchoate static on the crystal set.

The Christmas candle gutters between ravel and weave, between the invention and obsolescence of zero.

My father's ashes are in a jar in my sister's tool shed.

Over the harvested fields, the rain-wet marl of shadow clear to the stubble-frayed edge, the owl, rose-flecked by a cloud-smeared moon, as swift as the soul taking its leave, plunges down through the ruin: how else can a body stay alive, but to fall and rise as flesh: consumed, consuming, with brute relish.

I hung out at the Jesus freaks' coffee house. The House of Agape. Each night we were surprised and more than a little disappointed that the Rapture had not come. The coffee was awful, but the talk as hopeful as it must be on Death Row with appeal after appeal ahead. One night a nurse started speaking in tongues. She fell to the linoleum floor as if in a seizure, her right foot clanging against a metal folding chair. One of her garters unsnapped and danced on the white flesh of her upper thigh. After that night, I did not return.

The moth-eaten lacework of the moon, a dream calculus, inscribed yet unutterable, beyond solution.

When I asked where it is, he said, *My town is as far away from the next as near to anything.*

# The Education of the Poet

Before the Tigris and the Euphrates, before the sedimentary, igneous, and metamorphic rocks were labeled and set on a shelf behind a panel of glass that slid creakily on ball bearings, before negative numbers, before fractions, before the earth, tilted on its axis, moved close to the sun and thus, illogically, it was winter, before the tornado drill, the fire drill, duck and cover, before the venetian blinds were opened and the dust of all summer rose like dust into the light's slant, before the chairs were lifted one by one from the desks to the floor, before the protractor measured an acute angle on the board, before the compass, before the pocketknife flipped once and landed blade-first in the playground dirt in a game of mumblety-peg, before he pressed a chord button on the autoharp and a pick stumbled up music, the boy spoke the words, "I pray the Lord my soul to take, Amen," and his day ended. He said it sincerely, in the voice of one whose prayer, once rote, was now a spell of sorts, or a key, a lifted latch, the trapdoor through which he entered sleep. How light he felt at the disputed border of dream, as if something *had* been taken from him and he knew—the boy did not have the words for it yet—that *gravity* and *grace* would always be the variables, the integers and sum, the divisors and quotient, the end points of a single line, and to that end, the principle product of his brooding.

# The Blindfold

Because I wear a blindfold, I close my eyes. The dark is darker that way. That sound, like a rowboat in fog, is the attic fan. I try not to imagine the dust it blows around. If a room assumes the identity of those who inhabit it, this is my mother's room, or rather the room of my mother's ghost. By force of habit, the charred tree blooms in the yard. I do not see it. I am blindfolded. I catch in the air a scent like chalk erasers clapped together, the little plume that rises to the school janitor's nose and causes him to sneeze. How neatly he refolds his handkerchief and slips it into the unbuttoned pocket of his khaki work-shirt. My mother's ghost lights up a cigarette. A little shred of tobacco clings to her lip. She licks her finger and touches the hot iron. The inside of the cast iron frying pan is white with the congealed fat of morning bacon. On the TV, a gentleman vampire waits a long time before opening the door to the uninvited guest. Perhaps you find the blindfold an affectation. But only when I wear the blindfold and close my eyes do I hear the static of towels lifted from the basket, breathe an air of steam and starch, feel her brush past on some task, humming "Moon River" or "Sugar Town."

## Multiples of Twelve

What did I know then: the state capitals, the multiples of twelve, how a panther devours the liver first and then the heart? I remember my father's silhouette—rickety, dusk-burdened—in the doorway. He exhales and smoke blunts the hard edges. I am not sure who he was to me then except a tired man in a doorway watching crows pick apart the day's remains, the horizon's tree line spark, flare, and fade, his stubborn son, called in for the evening, taking his time, taking his own sweet time.

# The Convalescence

Drubbed by fever, all stupor, he wakes to the sound of his mother darning socks, to the little song the thread sings as it follows the needle.

A child deprived of the right words for things, he sees through to the verge of the invisible: dusk, beyond his window, puts down roots at the field's edge.

The wind paces between the open windows like a famished wolf. He cannot teach it patience. Its fur hackles at the slightest noise.

He is still young enough that his heart hangs where it should and not knotted between his legs. And yet how strange words *blouse* and *breast*.

A swarm of hornets burns in the attic above; dark water haunts the cellar below.

# Louie

After the first stroke, the father slurred his words and thus grew quiet. Memory is a revision, a recasting. The father had a friend, a drunk named Louie. He'd do anything for Louie. Once, the father and son bailed Louie out of jail. There was Louie freed from custody on the steps of the Raytown Police Station. "Louie, when did you grow a beard?" the father asked, each word clear, unmuddied by the stroke. What the boy saw before him was a man who wore as a mask a swarm of bees.

# The Magician's Suitcase

With an unfolded paperclip, the lock is easy enough to pick. Open and empty, the suitcase is like a body abandoned by its spirit. Closed, the suitcase takes on weight: chains, anvils, I-beams. . . . But unlatched and opened, it reveals merely a frail nest of hair pulled from a brush, a single nail clipping piercing the striped silk lining. Closed, a low-tide sludge leaks drop by drop from where the two halves join. For you, this opening and closing is like a game you played when your visited Aunt Eva and Uncle Martin, who were not your aunt and uncle, and were older than your grandparents, who had died before you were born. You would go from floor to floor in their mansion and each door opened onto a different room than it had upon your last visit. Only the elevator door opened onto the same space as you slid the folding brass cage-like door to the side and it disappeared into the wall. You open the suitcase and find a brand new white shirt with pins holding the tucked sleeve behind the shirtfront, cardboard stiff in the collar. You close the suitcase and hear a song within like a gamelan, like a pocketful of dimes dropped onto a ballroom's wooden floor. Opened: smoke rises as it does around a hive's dazed bees. Closed: it could be filled with anyone's dirty laundry packed haphazardly at the end of a trip cut short. Sometimes you crawl inside the suitcase and pull it shut. The space is not cramped at all. Sometimes the odor of camphor and paste wax reminds you of the empty attic floor where the elevator stopped. When the door opened, you would shout to hear your voice echo back distorted by the distance. But the suitcase is not the elevator, not a means of transport. To own the suitcase, you are burdened to lift it, to keep in your pocket as a key a paperclip.

# Home

We lived in a house of cards. For each of us to have a full hand, we had to remove the roof and two walls. Then rain got in. To see, we'd milk the viper's venom, but it released a feeble light, better for a séance than Texas Hold'em. The same pot redistributed night after night seemed once a fortune. Distracted by the bituminous dusk, trying to piece together the last verse of "Amazing Grace," I often lost at cards. During the day, in a department store dressing room, with strangers naked from the shins down, I'd practice my poker face in the tri-fold mirror. Some nights I came home to a wide, sprawling ranch house. Some nights to a rickety high-rise. Today, after high winds and tornado warnings, it was a lean-to of a sideways joker and an ace of clubs.

# The Mess

The newborn calf shakes off its caul as it stumbles and stands and standing wobbles (is it mud season? Indian summer?) and Doc Blackwell laughs and wipes the slime and muck onto his coveralls, lights up a Lucky Strike, (does he know by now I am fucking his daughter?) spits on the match and puts it in his pocket, shoos away the barn cats licking at the calf, (is the past a road that rises up at the end like a question?) tells me to clean up the mess.

## At the Party

You thought you were hearing a story, so the punch line, like bright sun after a long movie, caught you off guard. You laughed late and perhaps too earnestly at a party where you, an extra held down by the failed possibilities of the passing moment, were meant to blend in with others in the spare *mise-en-scene*.

Did you *RSVP*? Were you the uninvited guest scarfing the crab puffs, telling a joke wrung from the dry rag of the self? Or were you the host, tending to some wine stain in the rug, leaving your guests to the givens of gravity, the dead weight of small talk?

Everyone crowded into the kitchen and you, whoever you were, seemed a thing of glass—a vitrine—not invisible, but *see-through-able*: liver, lungs, and kidneys on display, not to mention the warp and buckle of bowels.

# Essay on Compassion

I caught a fox in a Havahart trap. When I went to release him,
he hunched, hissed, snapped, let out a yelp, and bared his teeth;
defending the corner I'd put him in. He stunk with a blunt odor of
musk and myrrh, a hint of shit. I had to shake him out of the cage
with more violence than I'd have preferred.

# Self-Portrait with Depression

There's a certain point in each evening when you forget the murky depth of your depression, how it lodges like a canker, like dross and slag where in others breath and blood abide; nonetheless, that point *is* a point upon which you can balance for only so long, so you focus all your energy on that center of gravity, and though to suffer loss without a lost object, to fidget among the plural answers to a single question, and to brood *are* your prerogatives and habits, you can for a moment and upon that point suspend the symptoms of your malady, and not kill time, the interval and duration, not annul the *now* and the *next*, and not exactly feel pleasure, per se, but feel, for now, the pleasure of its pursuit, as if you had cornered a quarry, and if one who did not know you took your picture in this instant, one might guess from it that you are a happy man, and if not a happy man, certainly a man on the verge of happiness, a man on whom something like a fleeting smile crosses, and whose eyes, bright in the flash, look out, and not inward, into the near, not too distant future, as you recall, for some reason, what Jean Dubuffet once said: *Art does not lie down on the bed that is made for it; it runs away as soon as one says its name; it loves to go incognito; its best moments are when it forgets what it is called,* and you remember you once had a name and at this hour from the front porch of your childhood home a man or a woman would stand in the evening shadows and call you home, and against your will you answered to that name and were called.

# Documentary Evidence

Fireflies amid sparse stars. The wind's splendid indifference, snagged in a bramble hedge. Mars, low on the horizon, like a spark in straw. The muddy ground attests to rain, but he remembers no rain. That it rained. He cannot remember the people in the photograph. Each of their names is written in pencil on the back of the photograph. Nonetheless, he cannot remember. The person closest in the picture points to something outside the frame, but the others beside her do not notice, caught off guard as they are by the flash. Mars, low on the horizon. The wind's splendid indifference, snagged in a bramble hedge. Fireflies amid sparse stars. Mars flares like straw afire. Asked to verify, all he can remember is what is not in the photograph.

# The Enigma of a Useless Key

One can say: *the sea like an empty house.* One can say: *for my days pass away like smoke.* One brings to the landscape one's own belatedness: a knowledge of wreckage, a wreckage of knowledge. One can say a spell against forgetting, against time. Time is not the subject but the drama. Time is not the drama but the stage. The years hang like curtains pleated, overlapping: *shadow-wells, bright edges.* The battlefield ravens are glutted, the orchard trees stooped with pears. Because one is *of* it, not *in* it, the wilderness is impenetrable.

# Exile and Return

Between exile and return, between cleft and crag: a narrow footbridge of smoke, a bolt of silk unfurled. The falconer stands as still as a saint in a fresco where the world is arcane and mineral, unmoved and unmoving. To reveal the strata of the senses as more than depthless replicas, more than trappings, the falconer lifts his gloved hand, and from between the *Book of the Sovereign* and the *Book of the Habitable Earth*, a falcon descends: how it lumbers and stalls mid-air before dropping its trove, before it perches on the outstretched hand and is hooded.

# Acknowledgments

Much of the work here appeared originally, often in earlier drafts, in the following journals. I am grateful to the generous attention of the editors of these publications for their insight, encouragement, and patience.

*Bat City Review, Chattahoochee Review, The Cimarron Review, The Cincinnati Review, The Controlled Burn, The Cortland Review, Delmar, Free Verse, The Georgia Review, Image, The Innisfree Poetry Journal, The Iowa Review, The Laurel Review, Limp Wrist, Memorius, Narrative, The New Orleans Review, Pleiades, River Styx, Rooms Outlast Us, Saint Katherine Review, Salamander, Sentence, Slope, Smartish Pace, So To Speak, Subtropic, The UCity Review*

This book is dedicated to the many graduate students over the past sixteen years at George Mason University who have taken my course on the history of the prose poem and whose challenging writing prompts led to the earliest drafts of many of these poems.

# About the Author

Eric Pankey is the author of nine previous collections of poetry, including most recently *The Pear as One Example: New and Selected Poems 1984–2008* and *Trace*. His work has been supported by fellowships from the Ingram Merrill Foundation, The National Endowment for the Arts, the Brown Foundation, and the John Simon Guggenheim Memorial Foundation. He is Professor of English and the Heritage Chair in Writing at George Mason University in Fairfax, Virginia, where he teaches in the MFA and BFA programs in Creative Writing.

Photograph of Eric Pankey by Rachel Eliza Griffiths. Used by permission.

# Free Verse Editions

Edited by Jon Thompson

*13 ways of happily* by Emily Carr
*Between the Twilight and the Sky* by Jennie Neighbors
*Blood Orbits* by Ger Killeen
*The Bodies* by Chris Sindt
*The Book of Isaac* by Aidan Semmens
*Canticle of the Night Path* by Jennifer Atkinson
*Child in the Road* by Cindy Savett
*Contrapuntal* by Christopher Kondrich
*Country Album* by James Capozzi
*The Curiosities* by Brittany Perham
*Current* by Lisa Fishman
*Dismantling the Angel* by Eric Pankey
*Divination Machine* by F. Daniel Rzicznek
*Erros* by Morgan Lucas Schuldt
*The Forever Notes* by Ethel Rackin
*The Flying House* by Dawn-Michelle Baude
*Instances: Selected Poems* by Jeongrye Choi, translated by Brenda
    Hillman, Wayne de Fremery, and Jeongrye Choi
*A Map of Faring* by Peter Riley
*Pilgrimly* by Siobhan Scarry
*Physis* by Nicolas Pesque, translated by Cole Swensen
*Poems from above the Hill & Selected Work* by Ashur Etwebi, translated
    by Brenda Hillman and Diallah Haidar
*The Prison Poems* by Miguel Hernández, translated by Michael Smith
*Puppet Wardrobe* by Daniel Tiffany
*Quarry* by Carolyn Guinzio
*remanence* by Boyer Rickel
*Signs Following* by Ger Killeen
*Summoned* by Guillevic, translated by Monique Chefdor
*These Beautiful Limits* by Thomas Lisk
*An Unchanging Blue: Selected Poems 1962–1975* by Rolf Dieter
    Brinkmann, translated by Mark Terrill
*Under the Quick* by Molly Bendall
*Verge* by Morgan Lucas Schuldt
*The Wash* by Adam Clay
*We'll See* by George Godeau, translated by Kathleen McGookey
*What Stillness Illuminated* by Yermiyahu Ahron Taub
*Winter Journey* [Viaggio d'inverno] by Attilio Bertolucci, translated by
    Nicholas Benson

CPSIA information can be obtained at www.ICGtesting.com
Printed in the USA
BVOW04s1122110115

382779BV00002B/42/P

9 781602 354876